EIGHT STEPS

To a fulfilling Life

A Simple, Direct Roadmap
That Can Help Anyone.

IMAGINATION PRESS

Teresa Hamilton

Editors
Doc Wilson
Ishmael Azizz
Victoria Moore
Cynthia Belcuore

Cover Design/Layout Artist
Francis Adams

Publisher
Imagination Press LLC

Eight Steps to a Fulfilling Life
A Simple, Direct Roadmap That Can Help Anyone!
by Teresa Hamilton

Second Edition

Printed in the United States of America
ISBN-13: 97809995209-9-4
Copyright © 2007 by Teresa Hamilton
All rights reserved.

No part of this book may be reproduced or utilized in any form or by any means, electronic, or mechanical, including photocopying and recording, without permission in writing from the publisher.

Contents

Dedication. 5
Forward. 7

SECTION I: INTERNAL PRINCIPLES. 9
   Chapter 1: PRINCIPLE 1:PURPOSE. 11
      Exercises. 16
   Chapter 2: PRINCIPLE 2: POSITIVE THINKING. 19
      Exercises. 24
   Chapter 3: PRINCIPLE 3: PRAYER. 25
      Exercises. 28

SECTION II: INTERNAL and EXTERNAL PRINCIPLES. 30
   Chapter 4: PRINCIPLE 4: PREPARATION 32
      Exercises. 37
   Chapter 5: INTERNAL and EXTERNAL PRINCIPLES. 39
   Chapter 6: PRINCIPLE 5: PRESSURE. 41
      Exercises. 46
   Chapter 7: PRINCIPLE 6: PERFORMANCE. 49
      Exercises. 52
   Chapter 8: PRINCIPLE 7: PASSING IT ON. 53
      Exercises. 57

SECTION III: PUTTING IT ALL TOGETHER. 59
   Chapter 9: PRINCIPLE 8: PEACE. 61
      Exercises. 64
      Epilogue. 65
   Notes. 66

Dedication

This book is dedicated to God, who has been my constant companion since I can remember. I've made a ton of mistakes along my journey to a fulfilling life, but the one constant has been my connection to Him. This book is also dedicated to my late mother, Louise Hamilton. I was fortunate to be her daughter. She was a God-filled woman who lived out her true purpose in the Lord. Lastly, I wish to dedicate this book to my father, Joseph Hamilton. My dad has supported me 100% all of my life by giving me unconditional love and support.

I also wish to thank all of my family. There is not one member of my family who has not gone out of their way to help me -- and on numerous occasions. A special thanks to my sister and brother in- law, Marie and Thomas Hardy, Jr.

Lastly, I wish to thank my "Making It Happen" group, the members of which have stood by me through the hard times, as well as the good ones. Specifically, I wish to thank Nargas Hyman for guiding me through the self-publishing maze. [By the way, if you would like to join this group, or just are curious about it, go to the website: imaginationpresslllc.com]

Forward

This book is based on the premise that God has given each of us a life blueprint to follow; and when we follow our God-given blueprint, we will lead more successful lives.

The goal of this book is to help you lead a more successful life by showing you how to employ the 8 principles that have helped me to be successful. I am 100% confident that you, too, will be highly successful in virtually every aspect of your life when you faithfully apply these 8 principles.

Purpose,
Positive Thinking,
Prayer, Preparation,
Pressure,
Performance,
Passing It On, and
Peace.

Let's begin the journey!

[ps: Feel free to give me your feedback on my website: www.imaginationpressonline.com]

SECTION I

INTERNAL PRINCIPLES

Chapter 1

PRINCIPLE 1

Purpose

Consideration of several **key questions** will help put you in the proper mindset for this chapter:

> Why are you here on earth?

> What does society require or expect of you?

> Are you certain that you are doing what you are supposed to be doing?

> Do you wish that you were in a different occupation?

> Do you feel that days pass on and on, but with, at most, only minimal emotional attachment from you?

These questions are designed to invoke aspects of your inner being that relate to "the purpose of life" itself -- **for you!** Fundamentally,

What Is *Your* Purpose?

My belief system and my life experiences indicate that you and I were given a **life blueprint** from God right from our beginning, i.e., from the moment we were pushed out of the womb. And your specific purpose in life will manifest itself when you keep in close contact with your Maker. Your specific purpose will then help determine the course (or at least the direction) of your life's journey.

God has given to you your specific **Purpose** to help you achieve your life goals.

Important Question:

How do you know whether you are pointed in the right direction?
The answer lies in whether you experience **"cognitive dissonance,"** a psychological term coined by Festinger. Essentially, "cognitive dissonance" means that the further you are from your life goals or life blueprint, the more dissonance or unhappiness you will feel. In other words, if you are not doing what you are destined to do in life, then you most likely will experience overt unhappiness, lethargy, depression, and/or listlessness.

Look at this issue another way:

How many illnesses (such as hypertension, anxiety disorders, and migraines) are due, at least in large measure, to people's unwillingness or inability to recognize that they are simply "going through the motions" in life, and not living up to their full potential? Or, how many cases of violence and abuse are the direct or indirect result of lives in which the perpetrators are just "going through the motions?"

So, how do you get on track to live up to *Your* **Purpose?** The key is simple and direct: you just need to get in touch with your Higher Being. If you have not established an ongoing dialog with God, do so, and include a series of questions along the following lines:

What am I supposed to be doing?

How would You like me to make a difference in the lives of others?

What path should I take?

Such questions will not offend God. On the contrary, God will enjoy your asking Him about *your* **purpose** in this world. Also, do not be alarmed if it takes a while to receive the full answer from Him. In particular, realize that sometimes God may give you one or more of the pieces of the puzzle that constitutes your life blueprint, and only later reveal the bigger puzzle pieces that will help make clear what your particular purpose and destiny are in life. -- Think of it this way: If God revealed your true, full purpose in life all at once, then you possibly would work entirely on your own to achieve your purpose and destiny -- without receiving His guidance or instruction along the way. Also, keep in mind that He may need to "fine tune" your plan from time to time, or require that you achieve certain milestones before graduating to the next step. So, apply patience, and just "go with the flow" that He prescribes for you.

Once you have established an ongoing dialog with God, you will be in a mental state to appreciate the following: **By relying on God to provide the purpose for your life, you will be much more effective, and accomplish far more in life than you could ever imagine.** In part, this is true because your human nature tends to limit your deeper thinking, for example, by leading you to base your thinking mainly on your past actions and experiences. In addition, your past failures too often may provide the basis for your actions and thoughts, whereas **strong focus on your past and present**

successes and your full potential will provide a healthier, incredibly more effective foundation for expanding your critical and creative thought processes.

Finally, there may be times when your life blueprint requires doing things that are not familiar or not comfortable; thus, relying on God can expand your horizons in (currently) unfathomable ways.

How to Find *Your* Purpose
Four daily exercises will help you find your specific purpose, or at least the starting point for your life journey of self discovery, including discovery of your life blueprint.

First, start by seeking God as your spiritual guide. As is indicated above, it may take a while to discern your true, full purpose (or your first step thereto), but you can facilitate matters by asking Him to reveal bits of the details here and there. For example, you might start by asking God to reveal the job(s)/profession(s) he wants you to perform. Realize that when you ask God for a job, He will provide you with the necessary skill sets to accomplish that job, or direct you to training/education to acquire those skill sets.

Second, make it a habit to read extensively -- not only the Torah, the Holy Bible, and the Koran, but also a variety of subject categories of books, for example, philosophy, history, biographies, etc. The ideas in such books will help shape and expand not only your specific thoughts and thought processes, but, additionally, the habitual act of seeking out such books at the library, bookstore, or on the Internet, etc., oftentimes miraculously will lead you to books on other topics that will prove to be critical to your mental and spiritual growth and development.

Third, always listen to the small, still voice that gives you insight and direction.

As you journey through life, realize that that small, still voice is **your compass** to help you make the right decisions in your life. You will be able to appreciate that the small, still voice is authentic because, when you listen, you will experience peace that is not momentary, but, rather, is permanent. See Chapter 9 for more on **Peace**.

Fourth, be mentally 100% clear that you will take your life's journey with absolutely no fear of failure -- because failure is *not* an option under God! Use daily expressions of positive affirmations to achieve this. Start by making certain that your life is pointed in the right direction, and then get to work! -- This prescription implies that you need to make an affirmative decision to **exclude negative thoughts** from your thinking and self-talk; i.e., don't waste time and energy on things that you know will not come to pass.

The last sentence implies that **you *do* have the power to control your thinking patterns, including your mood and general mental disposition.** This point is developed further in the next chapter: *Positive Thinking*. However, it is important to point out here one of the secrets used by top salespersons for decades: They start their business day with self-talk that includes **affirmations** about their capabilities, and what they will accomplish that day and that week, month, etc. If you are serious about life, you will do the same. Proper execution of this fourth step constitutes an **affirmation that you *will* accomplish your life blueprint -- i.e., you *will* fulfill your purpose in life.** Briefly, let's expand the "thinking patterns – mood – mental disposition" issue to fall within the broader concept of **mental health.** Though it is beyond the scope of this book, realize that, at a minimum, **your great mental health** requires *regular, over-the- long-haul* practice of **at least 5 things:**

8   great nutrition,

8   great aerobic exercise (and it has to be sufficiently demanding),

8   great strength-promoting exercise (and it has to be sufficiently

demanding),

8   sufficient deep sleep each night, and

8   adequate stress reduction if too much stress is present in your life.

[For a thorough, yet relatively brief treatise on this topic, including a broad expose of many of the myths in these five areas, consult **Total Health in a Nutshell** by Doc Wilson.] Having great mental health not only will contribute an important part to your overall good health in general, but it also will provide a firm foundation for **positive thinking**, which, in turn, will contribute significantly to success in your daily affirmation exercises.

Exercises

1. If you know Your Purpose, write it down.

----

2. If you don't know <u>Your Purpose</u>, jot down all of the things that you <u>really</u> enjoy doing.

....

....

....

....

....

....

....

....

....

....

....

....

....

Chapter 2

PRINCIPLE 2

Positive Thinking

Positive Thinking is <u>*a must*</u> to be truly successful in any and every aspect of your life. Many books have been written about positive thinking, including Norman Vincent Peale's perennial bestseller (even though he died in 1993) **<u>The Power of Positive Thinking</u>**. The main thrust of this book is the importance of thinking positively, and having faith in God to help each of us live a successful life.

Another example is the **<u>Holy Bible</u>.** One of my favorite passages is written by the Apostle Paul in Philippians, Chapter 4, Verses 8-12:

Whatever things are true, whatever things are honest, whatever things are noble, whatever things are just, whatever things are pure, whatever things are lovely, whatever things are of a good report, if there is any praise, think on these things.

You need to understand that specific and general circumstances are immutable and as they should be. Thus, **you must learn to routinely think positively**, as this is one of the absolute requirements for a fulfilling life. This is true even if, because of your positive attitudes, you are the "lone black sheep" in your family or in any group or business to which you belong.

Maintaining a positive attitude does not mean that you are a pushover -- incapable of seeing the world in a realistic light. Rather, it means that

1) whatever direction you take,

2) whatever decision that you make as a leader within an organization, or

3) however you take control of your life,

you will do so with the full expectation of only the best result(s) -- in spite of the negative attitudes of others around you. (Also, realize that some negative attitudes are rooted in positive human needs, such as self preservation: e.g., a conservative approach to a situation may be considered "safer" by some.) Of course, you will not always experience perfect results by simply maintaining a positive attitude. However, in the long run, **your consistently positive attitude** will help you achieve much better odds for a positive outcome.

Maintaining a positive attitude in the face of adversity is a skill that you can easily develop. One **key** to this process is to realize that **confidence that you are doing "the right thing" forms the basis for being able to forge ahead when others are doubting Thomases.** Another perspective on this process is to view adverse negativity that you encounter in your life as God testing or challenging you -- perhaps as a way to determine if you are ready to advance to the next step in your life blueprint. If you are unrelentingly complaining and grumbling (e.g., consider the biblical story of the Israelites in the wilderness), God may require a series of additional challenges or tests until you have developed the ability to **routinely ignore the negative, and embrace the positive**. Therefore, once you can routinely be thankful, content, and positive in the face of adversity, then God will step into your life with his supernatural power to move you forward to the next step toward achieving your ultimate destiny.

Many successful people will tell you that it was their personal faith, or their belief that something would turn their way, that helped them reach a major milestone, goal, or objective -- despite the

negative attitudes of family and friends saying such things as: "You can't do that." Or, "How are you going to feed yourself?" Or, as in the case of the Wright brothers, "No one has ever done that before; you must be totally crazy!"

Sooner or later (and the choice of timing is yours to make), in spite of all of the obstacles and detours that life delivers to your doorstep, you will learn that **you possess an inner drive that serves to steer you in a direction consistent with your life blueprint.** On the other hand, frequently you may find that you are almost robotic in many of your choices -- yielding to a "heard mentality" in which you follow the prescriptions of others. You can easily recognize such prescriptions of others because they usually fall within a commonly-held aphorism, such as "Go to school, get a degree, and find a good job." I believe that following such prescriptions, without proper inquiry or challenge, could promote mental and physical illness in your body. In addition, such prescriptions could promote cognitive dissonance within your psyche, which, as was discussed in <u>Chapter 1</u>, means that, most likely, you are not on the proper path to fulfilling your life blueprint.

Although the "Go to college and find a good job" prescription is a potentially good one in the sense that it could equip you for a solid position in our fast-paced, technological society, it is a flagrant example of a **one-size-fits-all mentality** that simply may not fit your psyche and your life blueprint. Also, you should never automatically adopt someone else's vocational (or other) prescription; rather, you should first make certain that you genuinely have an open mind, and then do some hard soul-searching, and possibly also some vocational testing. Then, finally (possibly also with a bit of determination, luck, and divine intervention), you will find that vocation that is consistent with your life blueprint.

To elaborate further, finding the vocation of your life blueprint can feel like peeling an onion: for example, **you may discover your destined vocation one layer at a time, particularly if your ultimate vocation is a multi-faceted one.** However, do not be surprised if finding the vocation of your life blueprint occurs

immediately. For example, consider basketball great Kobe Bryant, who always knew he was destined for professional basketball; or Bill Gates, who felt his calling in the information technology area so strongly that he dropped out of Harvard to pursue that dream on his own. On the other hand, do not be surprised if the process takes half of your life, or more. Your key to a successful ultimate outcome is to be patient, enjoy life and your current profession, and keep a positive attitude by realizing that **everything will work out in due time when you put your life in the hands of Him.**

How Do You Maintain a Consistently Positive Attitude Over the Long Haul?

You must practice **six key things** to maintain a positive attitude on a virtually-always basis.

First, make certain that you have a positive, ongoing relationship with God. Since God is the one who is directing the path of fulfillment of your life blueprint, have faith that He will lead you to an eminently successful outcome. Realize, too, that God will help lessen any anxiety that you may presently have (e.g., based on pressure from family and friends) because He has the ultimate control. Your life is in his kind, gracious hands.

Second, in both your personal life and your professional life, surround yourself with positive people whenever possible, and minimize your contact with negative people. Positive people will help your mental health and your attitude without their even knowing it.

Third, consistently provide genuine, extreme positivity toward _everyone_ with whom you come in contact. In other words, work hard to provide a positive influence on others, just as those who serve as your "positivity gang" in the second key above; i.e., do unto others as you would have them do unto you. Your rewards will be immeasurable.

Fourth, frequently (i.e., multiple times each day) practice the art of dismissing any and all of the negative thoughts that you carry within you -- though you may not be conscious of them. First, if your negative thoughts are subconscious, you must first learn to bring them to the surface so that you can recognize them. If necessary, solicit the input of your closest friend or two. Second, realize that **your ultimate success almost always has absolutely _no_ bearing on any past mistakes that you or anyone else ever made --except in cases in which you have _learned_ from such mistakes.** Third, **fill your mind with positive thoughts and positive images, fill the walls of your work space and your private space with positive sayings, and positive photos and works of art, and Let your imagination soar unfettered from time to time, for these will crowd out most of the negatives.** Fourth, if there is an unresolved negative in your past that concerns another person(s), and that weighs mightily on your mind, confront that person(s) in an appropriate way that at least brings an improvement in your mental state -- if not a total resolution.

Fifth, as indicated earlier, remind yourself daily of your great qualities and your great potential for good by making affirmations that emphasize those traits.

Sixth, no matter how bad your present circumstances may be (or may become), realize that it is a _temporary_ status, and that, sooner or later, you _will_ work through it and be better off thereafter.

Follow this **six step roadmap**, and you just may surprise not only yourself and your friends, but the entire world! In addition, you will improve the function of your immune system so that your risks for cancer are diminished appreciably.

```
1   2   3   4   5   6   7   8   9   10
O   O   O   O   O   O   O   O   O   O
```

Exercises

1. Score yourself on a scale of 1 to 10 (where 10 is the highest/best) as to how positive you are.

....

....

2. If your score is not an 8 or higher, write down what changes you need -- and would be willing to make -- in order to become a more positive person. If your score is an 8, 9 or 10, do the same thing if you believe that the process would be beneficial to you.

....

....

....

....

Chapter 3

PRINCIPLE 3

Prayer

As is true for everyone else, you have experienced the "highs," the "lows," and the numerous challenges of life. However, you may have missed applying one of the most powerful stabilizing forces that can help modulate your "seesaw of life" so that your swings are not as dramatic: **Prayer**. In addition to modulating your life swings, regular prayer will calm your spirit, and permit you to tap into your Higher Power.

Regular prayer will help you to affirm your desires and wishes, and to be better focused and directed toward achieving your life blueprint. When you make supplications to God, He will release his supernatural power to move you in the direction of fulfilling your life goals and objectives. Regular prayer will also help you to deal more effectively with stress and other of life's difficulties.

Do not expect prayer to make difficult situations disappear; however, **it is reasonable to expect prayer to help spur you forward in the direction of fulfilling your life blueprint.** Note that praying to your Higher Power will not absolve you of your duty to make intelligent decisions about how to conduct your life; on the contrary, **regular prayer will provide you with greater insight on how best to resolve**

a problem, reach a goal, or create a better world. In fact, God will have higher expectations for you -- compared to someone who is not highly spiritual.

As you work regular prayer into your life (if you have not already), **expand your subject matter to include people you see and meet, including the homeless beggar, as well as world leaders, and perpetrators of heinous crimes.** And be certain to include your friends who may be going through difficult times. Also, do not hesitate to pray for such things as better conditions for various cultures around the world, political issues, and the plight of endangered species.

Some believe that you will achieve even greater efficacy by **combining fasting with prayer.** For example, some claim that you will find it easier to break a bad habit (such as smoking or use of illicit drugs) when you combine fasting with prayer. However, *for medical safety, do not fast more that 48 hours at a stretch,* **for such negative effects as loss of muscle protein, etc., can occur with longer periods. And** *do not do more than one 48 hour fast in a given month for best medical results; and total fasting hours in a given month should not exceed about 60 hours.*

Old Testament history records the acts of the Israelites, who combined fasting with prayer in order to subdue their enemies and conquer their promised land. In the New Testament, Apostle Paul fasted and prayed that Christ's message would be well received not only by the Jews, but also by the Gentiles; subsequently, Christianity spread throughout the world. In the Muslim religion, Mohammed fasted and prayed that man learn to submit only to God, and not be swayed by various off-target sects; as we know, there are now over one billion Muslims around the world.

Tips on Praying
You can engage in prayer practically anywhere: in a quiet place in your home, in an elevator, in the shower, in a crowd, while enjoying a

movie or play (these might be more likely to be short prayers), while watching athletic competition, etc. You can pray with your eyes open or shut. Actually, there are no absolute rules as to when or how you choose to pray. However, I recommend that you pray at least twice a day -- perhaps once in the morning, and once over your lunchtime or in the evening.

You may experience times when you find yourself with no "pressing issues" about which to pray. In such cases, use your prayer time to meditate, and listen to that "small, still voice" that was identified in Chapter 1 as a source for insight and direction in your life.

As was discussed above, be certain to develop the habit of **thinking expansively** about the topics about which your praying is directed -- i.e., pray about more than just yourself and your family. **Think of praying for others as one of the most loving things that you can do.** Also, consider the added power of groups praying together on a given topic -- sort of a "squeaky wheel gets the grease" concept.

Finally, for really onerous difficulties (such as breaking a very bad or dangerous habit), consider combining fasting with prayer up to twice a week; however, keep in mind that you should impose an upper limit of *no more than 48 hours for a single fast, no more than 48 hours total for a single week, no more than one 48 hour fast in a month, and no more than a total of about 60 hours in a given month,* as was discussed above.

Exercises

1. List the desired events and your goals that have yet to materialize in your life.

----

2. List at least three people with whom you could pray on a daily or other frequent basis.

----

3. Starting with the three (or more) people listed above, establish a prayer circle that will meet one or more times a week.

SECTION II

INTERNAL and EXTERNAL PRINCIPLES

Chapter 4

PRINCIPLE 4

Preparation

Your life may often be complex -- including highly complicated schedules. One way you can reduce (at least somewhat) such complexity is to maximize your preparation for whatever life *specifically* is likely to throw your way (e.g., based on your chosen job, profession, or avocation); in addition, you can prepare in a *general* way for some of those unforeseeable "curve balls" that life also is likely to impose on you from time to time. Keep in mind that one purpose of great preparation is to ensure that you are prepared to the greatest extent possible when opportunity happens to knock.

The following **five steps** will help you better prepare for execution of your life blueprint.

First, the best starting point for **Preparation** is to **make certain that your mindset is always in a learning mode.** Examples of learning modes include reading, talking with and listening to others, and traveling. By habitually being in a learning mode (which, among other things, implies constant curiosity), you will find that life itself will not only be more interesting, but also you will be more firmly engaged in whatever task you have at hand. In addition, people will find you to be more interesting, and you will find others to be more interesting than you found them before. Finally, the combination of constant curiosity -- combined with intelligent choices about strategic issues and questions to raise in your preparation phase, will lead you to important and unexpected benefits, including "good contacts" and such things as information important for your current or next project or business.

Second, to get to the next step of your life blueprint, **be certain to practice relevant patterns of thought and action so that you can improve your "presentation" of pertinent subject matter or be a better executer of certain actions.** That sounds rather abstract, so let's look at several examples. Consider an actress who needs to practice her craft until the "big break" occurs, such as taking acting classes, working with an acting coach, working with a voice coach to perfect various accents, and going on casting calls (whether or not there is any chance of landing the job) to meet people in the business, and to learn some of the different formats and methodologies used for sizing up and grading actors who have shown up.

Another example would be an athlete working to improve his/her execution of their chosen sport -- for example, a "Michael Jordan" working year after year to become the best all-around basketball player to date. Note that Michael Jordan's dedication and passion more than made up for his not having the highest level of natural talent, and helped propel him to the super-star status he ultimately earned. -- A side note on Michael Jordan: Early in his career, he was often criticized by sports writers for various areas of weakness. Rather than reacting in "typical" human fashion (e.g., being recalcitrant, obstinate, and dismissive of such criticism as being incorrect or inaccurate), Michael accepted the criticism as being valid, and then worked extra hours to achieve perfection -- or at least something very close to perfection.

Third, be sure that you have the discipline and drive to follow through to completion. Frequently, one of the key elements missing from the lives of those who do not attain their hopes, dreams, and desires is **preparation.** -- If you want something badly enough, you will find a way to obtain it; but save yourself a of time and grief by creating and following an intelligent, appropriate plan -- such as is outlined in this book. And be sure to **build in time (daily, weekly, yearly, etc.) for adequate preparation.** Realize, too, that part of preparation is **mentally schooling yourself to have the discipline, drive, and mental**

toughness to routinely follow tasks through to completion; and be certain to apply this principle to your entire life blueprint. As was discussed in Chapter 1, use daily affirmations to help this process along.

Fourth, when you are preparing for a vocation, hobby, or other hope, dream, or desire, do not be afraid of failure; rather, view "failure" as one of your learning tools. In our success- and winning-obsessed society, too often there is room only for "success." However, do not embrace such shallow, limited thinking patterns. Instead, think about many of the top scientists and inventors who achieved success through a limited series of "failures," via which they learned what to do and what not to do. In addition, many top scientists have made important, serendipitous discoveries by not following "conventional wisdom." In other words, **dare to be different in your thinking whenever you have a reason that you believe overcomes "conventional wisdom" or "the usual pattern of thinking"** about a given topic.

Fifth, by being mentally prepared for obstacles, you will be more likely to experience the better one of two possible paths:

   a) if you select the right path, you will learn from your "failures";

   b) on the other hand, if you select the wrong path, you will most likely continue to repeat the same mistake(s), and become frustrated and unhappy.

If you find that you tend to repeat the same mistake(s) over and over, then consider the possibility (probability?) that you are not optimally pursuing your life blueprint, and refresh your memory about the discussion on "cognitive dissonance" in Chapter 1.

Another way of looking at this fifth step is to think about an old saying: **Insanity** is doing the same thing over and over, and expecting a different result.

Sometimes, it may be difficult to assess whether your **Preparation** is on-target to lead you to your desired success. For example, consider the tortuous path that Albert Einstein followed to develop the theory of relativity, or Brownian motion physics, etc. Initially, his fellow physicists considered his ideas to be preposterous. However, his dogged pursuit of deeper thinking and re-thinking of "conventional wisdom" in these areas of physics allowed him to overcome many obstacles and "failures"; yet, in the end, he achieved unprecedented stature in his discipline to the extent that he is universally regarded as an intellectual giant. [And we need not dwell on his shortcomings, such as his frequent habit of putting checks he received on the mantle, and never cashing them; and his failing elementary math classes early in his schooling (actually, he was far ahead of his classmates, and just found it hard to focus on the boring, easy math)].

Note that Einstein's preparation and passion figured heavily in keeping his life journey on track.

You can gain a sense of Einstein's thinking from one of my favorite quotations of his: I want to know God's thoughts... the rest are details.

Einstein was best known for laying the foundation for harnessing atomic energy. However, a lesser known contribution was his role in establishing the Jewish state of Israel. I believe that God orchestrated Einstein's life so that his success peaked just when it was needed most

-- i.e., when a person of his stature was needed to help establish a homeland for the Jews.

How Do You Best Prepare?

Let's dissect the case of a person who wants to become a writer.

If you are truly interested in becoming a great writer, you will prepare by immersing yourself in one or more ways in the field of writing. Obvious possibilities include such activities as attending and participating in creative writing classes, reading biographies about successful writers, interviewing successful writers, reading books in your areas of interest, joining groups directed to fostering the skills of writers, writing books, submitting books and other writings for publication, and asking different people in your community (and even in other communities) to read and critique your writings (including asking people you have never met: it doesn't take guts to approach strangers, it just takes confidence and resolve to optimally and maximally advance your skills whenever possible).
And keep in mind the old adage… Practice makes perfect!
However, it is best not to do this by blindly writing and writing and writing without the input of someone else who can ably critique or otherwise help you advance your writing skills.

Finally, consider the competitive edge that golfer Tiger Woods achieves by practicing virtually every day. Since golf is a "skill" game, for most practical purposes a golfer is playing against himself or herself every time they play the game. The same principle applies to the writer:

Learn to "play against yourself" as a way of preparing to be a great writer.

Exercises

1. List at least 3 short term goals that relate to your life blueprint as you currently perceive it; if you have no idea what your life blueprint is or might be, list at least 3 <u>short term</u> goals that relate to something you really love to do.

----

2. For your list for Exercise number 1, list at least 3 <u>long term</u> goals.

----

3. For each of the items you have listed for the above two Exercises, write a paragraph or two describing what you need to do to reasonably and rationally prepare for them.

Chapter 5

INTERNAL AND EXTERNAL PRINCIPLES

The principles of Chapters 1 through 4 are *internal* in nature. These principles require that you be actively engaged in asking questions of your Maker, and attempting to answer such questions as your purpose in life. In order to achieve optimum results, you also must work to maintain a positive attitude, routinely pray to God, and take appropriate *general* steps to prepare for life, as well as *specific* steps, such as preparing for a particular job or profession. These principles are *internally* driven, including, for example, your choices of what to pray for, and what job to prepare for.

The next three principles are *external* in nature, and require that you deal with issues or people outside of yourself.

For example, in real life, you might be challenged with **Pressures** that originate outside of yourself, including such possibilities as a death in your family, losing your job due to downsizing of the company for which you work, having to deal with a family member with substance abuse problems, or having to take care of yourself, a friend, or a family member with a potent illness, or otherwise deal with the various effects of the illness.

Successful achievement of your life blueprint also will require specific **Performances** by you -- often including obtaining **defined, tangible measures** of such performances. Examples of defined, tangible measures could include obtaining a bachelor's degree, learning a script for an acting part in a play or movie, or improving your free-throw percentage.

The third external principle requires you to **Pass It On** to others the knowledge, lessons, skills, and wisdom that you have learned throughout your life. In other words, you must gladly and readily share your talents and your wise perspectives with others you know and meet who are in need.

The eighth and final principle is **Peace**, which is both an internal and an external principle. As will be detailed in Chapter 9, you will obtain peace once you are able to effectively, routinely, and often simultaneously employ all of the preceding seven principles. Once you have obtained **Peace**, you will be well on your way to obtaining the state of "nirvana of your soul."

Chapter 6

PRINCIPLE 5

Pressure

Pressure is something that you may experience virtually every day. For example, you may feel pressure from an upcoming exam, unpaid bills, loss of a job by you, a friend, or a family member, loss of life or health by a loved one, uncertainty in a relationship with a "significant other," major injury to a friend from a terrible accident, being yelled at by your boss, being behind on a school or work project that has a fast-approaching deadline, etc.

Learning how to cope with such pressures is a measure of your overall ability to manage your life. If you do not have such coping skills, do not worry, for you will be able to develop them, or greatly improve the skills that you do have. Just follow these **8 guidelines**.

First, whenever it is within reasonable, "doable" limits, **choose actions that will prevent or diminish the impact of future potential headaches.** Examples include paying bills and traffic tickets on time, starting studying for a hard exam early on; making reservations for the office Christmas party well in advance, alerting your supervisor of a mistake that may be mitigated by prompt action, and other similar actions that will alleviate potential negative outcomes. An example of prompt action is having your supervisor talk appropriately with an inappropriately irate customer to preempt them before the source of agitation leads to festering into something major -- such as a law suit.

Second, if your schedule and your life are so hectic that you cannot routinely follow the first guideline, at least plan and schedule as far ahead as possible so that you diminish as many potential negative impacts on your life as you can. View the first guideline and this one as "cutting-them-off-at-the-pass" types of life tactics. These two guidelines are reminiscent of the old adage: "an ounce of prevention is worth a pound of cure"; and you will experience the wisdom of this adage and these two guidelines increasingly the busier you become. -- Following these prescriptions is not always going to be easy; however, this would be an appropriate place to refresh your memory about the discussion on **discipline and drive** under the third step in Chapter 4.

Third, when things become too stressful (perhaps even overwhelming), have a heart-to-heart talk with your best friend or a caring colleague at work. Have you ever noticed how quickly major concerns and issues seem to melt away when you talk things over with someone? Getting another's viewpoint often helps to put things and life into a better perspective.

Fourth, when things become really, *really* bad (and hopefully well before this point), remember to consult Him through prayer or discourse. Think of this as maintaining at least this one aspect of your spiritual life. Even if you give only 15 or 30 seconds here and there to such consultation, it will reap significant rewards for you as time marches on. I believe that God has provided you with **Fruits of the Spirit**, and that those fruits help you deal with the daily and the long- term pressures of life. The **Fruits of the Spirit** include love, joy, peace, gentleness, goodness, faith, meekness, humility, self-control, and good humor. I believe that whenever someone is so deeply troubled that they abuse such substances as food, drugs, and alcohol, it is at least in part because they have not fully exercised these fruits.

To expand on two particular **Fruits of the Spirit** -- love and self control, consider Dr. Martin Luther King's use of non-violent tactics to counter racial hatred that was slowly eroding the fabric and foundation of the American culture. His use of non-violent tactics was considered bizarre by a large part of the American society

because many people were used to fighting back when confronted with people trying to hurt them. However, King's tactics implied forgiveness and true love for all people -- including those so misguided that they would attempt to hurt those of a different skin color. Ultimately, King's tactics saved millions of others, though they contributed to his losing his own life prematurely. -- It is entirely possible that America would have taken a different path were it not for King's stand in favor of love and self-control.

Fifth, think about the possibility that the pressure you experience is a part of God's grand plan for you. Even though it may feel as if "it is you alone against the whole world," God may be molding and moving you toward fulfillment of your life blueprint. Think of this as part of the **development of your inner being** to bring out your full potential. In addition, by proving to yourself that you are able to weather such pressure, you are then in a better position to counsel others who have to deal with pressure-filled circumstances.

Sixth, consciously focus on the *"near-100%-probability"* that, once you get past your present crisis (or string of crises), you *will* survive (and hopefully be more or less intact!), and things *will* get much better thereafter! In other words, **practice the discipline of applying solid logic to more clearly perceive your present reality.**

Seventh, realize that you are not alone in facing heavy pressure, for dealing with pressure is one of the greatest challenges of life on earth -- including not only for humans, but also for all other

animals and sometimes even plants. One of the effects of stress is the body's production of the stress hormone cortisol, as well as other hormones and chemicals. The production of stress hormones has even been observed in such simple and common activities as a trout fighting to maintain its feeding spot or home in a stream in the face of an invading trout. In humans, high cortisol levels cause accumulation of anterior abdominal fat when, simultaneously, excessive calories are consumed; and the medical literature is replete with studies of the many resulting negative effects on the human body from such fat accumulation -- including greatly increased risks for many kinds of cancer, type 2 diabetes, and the cardiovascular diseases [such as strokes, Alzheimer's, heart attacks, high blood pressure, deep vein thrombosis, peripheral vascular disease, metabolic syndrome (syndrome X), etc.].

Eighth, be certain to maintain close-to-optimum nutrition and exercise programs during prolonged periods of stress and pressure, as well as throughout your life in general. Such programs during stressful periods will markedly diminish the degree of severity of any negative effects that otherwise might occur in your body, and, when practiced routinely, will greatly reduce your risks for contracting many cancers, cardiovascular diseases, and type 2 diabetes... (Again, as recommended in <u>Chapter 1</u>, consult Doc Wilson's **<u>Total Health in a Nutshell</u>** for an authoritative treatise on these areas.) On the exercise front, **be sure to schedule at least 2, and preferably 3, demanding workouts each week; and schedule one day off between each workout to allow your muscles to recover.** It is far better to have 3 demanding workouts – with a day off between each workout -- than 4, 5, 6, or 7 low-level workouts each week. (Note that this guideline contradicts a popular myth that is perpetrated by various U.S. government agencies, and by non-governmental organizations and unknowledgeable individuals.) And you do not need to expend a long time with each workout; 30 to 40 minutes of a great routine will suffice, though 50 to 80 minutes would be better on weeks or days when you have more time. A subtopic of exercise is: **get up and <u>*move*</u> (even if only for a minute or so) every 45 to 90 minutes.** This simple act will help clear the cobwebs from your mind and also decrease the probability that your body will produce deep vein thromboses, which could prove deadly. Thus, **on your in-between (recovery) days, as well as on your exercise days, be absolutely certain that you are not totally sedentary for any extended period of time.**

And don't forget nutrition, because **great nutrition will supply your body with all of the 40-some essential nutrients that your body needs for optimum function, including optimum function of your immune system to reduce the risks of many cancers, infections, type 2 diabetes, and cardiovascular diseases.** -- Also, keep in mind that, on average, each and every day your immune system works to ward off 10,000 cancers that attempt to establish a toehold in every cell in your body!

More Tips to Help You Handle Pressure Better

How you handle stress reflects how the internal parts of your body (physical, mental, and spiritual) function in response to pressure. In addition to the above 8 guidelines, for full or partial relief, **ask yourself questions** such as these:

1. Do my mind and spirit fully embrace the direction God has mapped out for me?

2. Do my mind and spirit maintain a positive attitude in spite of current circumstances that, on the surface, seem to indicate the presence of much negative energy in my life?

3. Have I been praying and preparing for my upcoming task(s)?

4. In essence, am I frequently checking my internal clock to make certain that I am responding appropriately to the external pressures of my life?

Lastly, whenever you have stress or pressure, **hold onto your faith that God is working for your overall good** -- even though His intentions for you may not be clear at present. By consciously maintaining such a stance, you will find that your emotions and feelings will be much better stabilized -- no matter what your present circumstances are, and no matter how horrific those circumstances might be. This is not to say that you will not cry or be sad from time to time; rather, through even the most difficult times, God will give you supernatural rest and strength to endure any pain and anguish that you may experience (but be certain to do your part in the exercise and nutrition areas!).

Also, if you have not already, learn to draw on the **Fruits of the Spirit** when you are going through difficult times, which ability will help you immensely become closer to a **perpetual state of overall Peace** -- especially including your inner-most self.

Exercises

1. List 3 things in your life that make you feel overwhelmed.

- -

- -

- -

2. For each item, list all of the major changes that you can make to help reduce the pressure or stress in your life.

----

3. Create a schedule for making each of those changes.

----

4. Finally, dig deep to create the mindset (resolve, drive, etc.) to guarantee success in making all of the changes you listed in Exercise Number 2

Chapter 7

PRINCIPLE 6

Performance

Performance is different from Preparation in that, with Performance, you are constantly keeping score, or keeping some sort of tally of your goals and objectives, to ensure that your goals are met. On the other hand, Preparation is what you are doing daily to remain in a state of readiness for life's journey. Since you must perform in order to live, how well you perform can be considered a measure of how well you are living your life.

Use the following 8 guidelines to ensure that your Performance progress is maximized.

First, to optimize your Performance, you must have a written plan. This is critical to your ultimate success. The process helps better define *your* vision, and your odds for total success. Writing your Goals and keeping them in a place for easy future reference will not only help them materialize much faster, but also unleash your inner power to move decisively forward in the right direction. -- In this context, recall the Biblical statement that people without a vision will perish.

Second, as you create your written plan, be certain not to go so fast that you do not fully think things through. This might include writing a first draft, and then allowing it to sit for a day or two, or even a week or more, before reviewing it for needed additions and updates; and this process might go through several iterations before you achieve a thorough, acceptable overall plan.

Third, be sure to include both short- and long-term goals in your plan. For example, if you were a high school junior planning to become a lawyer, you would know that that your short term goals would include successfully completing high school, attending and passing all of the degree requirements at an accredited college, and taking and passing the LSAT (the law school entrance exam). Your longer-term goals would include attending and passing an accredited law school, and passing the bar exam.

Fourth, generally, optimum Performance requires identifying a <u>tangible, measurable standard</u> by which to gage your Performance as to meeting or not meeting a particular goal. For example, if you wanted to become a jazz musician, you know that you would need to practice playing many jazz scores -- the specific number being a function of your playing abilities, which, in turn, would change as the level of your jazz playing abilities improved.

Another example of a <u>tangible, measurable standard</u> relates to overcoming a bad habit -- in this case, stopping smoking. If you currently were smoking a pack a day, your first goal might be to smoke only half a pack each day by the end of next week. Your second goal might be to cut your smoking to just a quarter of a pack by the end of the following week -- and so forth until you reached zero cigarettes a day.

Fifth, identifying and establishing Performance Standards can prove overwhelming for some -- even for the simplest of tasks. For example, consider the daunting task of "spring cleaning" your sizable home. A highly effective way to meet this challenge is to employ a divide-and-conquer strategy -- i.e., breaking the huge task into a series of smaller tasks, each having its own <u>tangible, measurable standard</u>. Thus, you might set up a schedule for cleaning each room in a particular order. Or, if painting walls

and ceilings were a part of "spring cleaning" in some rooms, you might first paint the rooms in a particular order, followed by cleaning blinds and shades, cleaning the surfaces of tables and dressers, and cleaning the floors and carpets.

Sixth, for some, a task greater than establishing Performance Standards is that of <u>Getting Started</u>. In this arena, you may find that your mind plays tricks on you. For example, it might be difficult to ascertain whether your difficulty in Getting Started is rooted more in "fear of failure," anticipation of boredom, distaste for physical effort, or a perception of more important things that need to be done at home or work.

With respect to the common "fear of failure" reason, be aware that your society and/or parents may not have prepared you to deal adequately with "failure" -- whether real or imagined. If you believe that much of your life is driven by a "fear of failure," my advice is to own up to any such failure(s), and then learn from it (them) so that you do not repeat it (them).

Seventh, learn to think clearly and accurately about your failure(s). For example, if you failed an exam, that would not automatically make *you* a "failure" or a "bad person"; rather, it might simply mean that you need to spend more time studying that subject, studying in a non-distracting environment, or working with a good tutor. So, don't beat up on yourself by jumping to unwarranted and unsupported conclusions!

Eighth, if you want to relatively quickly achieve the goals necessary to fulfilling your life blueprint; whenever possible surround yourself with positive friends, mentors, and teachers who, ideally, have done things similar to your aspirations. Their insights will unlock opportunities that you might never imagine, and you will be able to learn from *their* mistakes!

Exercises

1. To help gage progress over time, detail your short- and long-term goals on paper or on your computer in a way that will facilitate future comparisons.

----

2. List the names of at least 3 people who will help you achieve your goals.

Chapter 8

PRINCIPLE 7

Passing It On

I concur with those who believe that **a good measure of a person is how much positive impact they have on others** -- including those less fortunate (financially, socially, etc.). One of your most important missions on Earth is to help those who are less fortunate, or who need help in an area where you can help.

One of the unique characteristics of humans is their ability to be social at a very high level. Many other animals are social, too, but theirs is more of a rote or neurally preprogrammed behavior pattern: for example, consider ants and bees as good representatives of insects that are highly social; in addition, fish, birds and mammals exhibit genetically programmed social behavior patterns. Each of these animal groups, including humans, have societies in which survival of their members requires teamwork and cooperation among the various subgroups of members. For humans, it is not hard to understand that failure of society members to work cohesively as a group could result in the eventual eradication of mankind -- just consider what could happen if atomic weapons fell into the wrong hands!

You will find (if you have not already) that **when you pass on to others the wisdom, perspectives, and talents that you have developed over your life, you will feel a surge of joy.** Interestingly, many perceive that they receive more contentment, satisfaction, and pleasure from performing a kind or generous act than the recipient(s) of their act.

Passing on to others the benefits of your life experiences should include not only kind "physical" acts, but also kind words that are delivered verbally, on paper, or via the Internet. If you are routinely highly observant, you have noticed (perhaps even daily!) numerous **public acts of unkindness**. Sometimes the unkindness is relatively subtle, such as, over time, slowly destroying a person's reputation through the simple act of spreading and/or not challenging unsubstantiated gossip. At other times, the unkindness may be relatively direct and obvious, as in certain cases of public physical and/or mental abuse. On the other hand, a portion of the American society also has a tendency to view some people's kind words and acts with a degree of suspicion; perhaps those with jaundiced perceptions are just wary about the genuineness of the acts of some.

When you think back on your earlier years, chances are that you had one or more **mentors** who earnestly believed in you, and passed on to you helpful tips and other information that helped speed up your mental, psychological, and/or spiritual maturation processes. Your **mentor(s)** may have been someone from a job, from your family or your family's general social circle, from your church, synagogue or mosque, or from your school. In sports, it may have been a school coach or other member of the athletic department who guided you toward good life principles, and athletic principles applicable to your sport(s). Such coaches and staff may have helped you to become a star not only athletically, but also academically.

When you pass on the benefits of your life experiences to others, it is important to be certain that you do so with **the right heart and spirit** -- i.e., with the right attitude and the right mindset. You do not want to be, or perceived to be, a self-righteous, ignorant, know-it-all, or an arrogant jerk. You may discover, as I have, that people who are sincere in giving needed advice tend to make a strong, lasting impression. You can and will do the same.

Be certain that you **do not let your ego become involved when you help another person -- for that can lead to inappropriate, twisted perceptions and behaviors.** Further, you should never worry about the possibility that the person you help may, for example, surpass you in the chain of command in your workplace, or about the possibility of losing your job; for **it is your moral imperative to help others** - per God. **Proceed as if all will be OK in the end, and it _will_ become so!**

You need to **assume the role of mentor** in the lives of those with whom you come in contact -- if they are in need of such mentoring. Stories of the rich and famous are loaded with examples of individuals who stress how **_just one_ person in their lives made a huge, positive difference in the direction and outcome of their lives.** Others have reported two or three key persons who made the difference between a so-so life, and a great life. -- It's **all about showing a firm, resolute, totally positive belief in the talents and capabilities of another person. That is how you must pass it on!** (And absolutely _no_ **negatives are allowed in the process of your passing it on to another in need!)**

Other Tips On How to "Pass It On"

The Hebrew language contains the word "anamie," which means that each of us possesses a bit of God in us. To be explicit about the implications of this, **consider yourself to be playing the role of God when you help someone in need.** And recall the caring, well-chosen words of Jesus:

Even as you do so unto the least of these my brethren, you do so unto me.

Notice that these words contain no mention of consideration being given to whether you might be taken advantage of. So, do not waste any energy debating whether you will "get involved" with someone in need of your help. Just "do your thing" to pass it on. If you find this uncomfortable, realize that such feelings will be short- lived, and most likely will not occur once you have carried out your

work with two or three such persons in need. Actually, you will find that the opposite will occur: **you will experience a happier, more fulfilling life once you make "passing it on" a permanent part of your daily routine.** -- Realize, too, that a strong tradition of "passing it on" has existed in most cultures for thousands of years. Indeed, all of the people who have passed on their knowledge, talents, and financial blessings over the eons have helped mankind to survive, and even flourish.

The final point on "Passing It On" deals with **your spirit.** When your physical body eventually passes on, what will remain is your sharing, caring, giving spirit -- which will impassion others to do the same. If this seems too abstract or too unlikely, just think about the reasons we celebrate Martin Luther King' birthday, Gandhi's life, or John D. Rockefeller's philanthropy, or about why so many talk incessantly about Oprah Winfrey. Each of these individuals possesses a heart that is powerfully and caringly directed to helping others. Their lives are supreme examples of the good that can result from passing it on to others. Though your life *may* not provide as high a profile impact as theirs (then again, your life *might well!* -- so don't make any unwarranted assumptions about such things!), keep in mind that **"passing it on" is a condition of your heart and your spirit; and if your heart and your spirit are in the right place, you cannot help but pass it on!** -- for your heart and spirit will impassion others to do the same.

I sincerely hope that you fully appreciate that **I am counting on <u>YOU</u> to set new standards on how richly one may <u>Pass It On</u> to others in need!**

Exercises

1. Write down the names of at least 3 people that you currently know who could benefit from your "passing it on" to them.

....

....

....

2. Create a list of ways you can volunteer to help others in your immediate community, and elsewhere -- e.g., worldwide via the Internet.

....

....

....

....

....

SECTION III:

PUTTING IT ALL TOGETHER

Chapter 9

PRINCIPLE 8

Peace

You will have obtained total inner **Peace** when you feel completely at ease -- despite your current adverse circumstances (if any). In other words, you are at **Peace** when you are detached from the cares (real or imaginary) of the world.

One of my favorite quotes regarding peace is from the **Holy Bible:**

Be anxious for nothing, but in everything by prayer and supplication with thanksgiving, let your requests be made until God and the peace of God which passes all understanding shall keep your hearts and minds through Jesus Christ.

This passage means that when you place your trust in God, you can relax -- knowing that, regardless of any obstacles or problems, He will guide your life in a supernatural way to achieve the best result(s) for you.

Maintaining your inner **Peace** in the American society is difficult at best. This is true partly because the society has so many people whose value systems do not empower or help others; rather, their value systems tend to tear people down. For example, individuals who embrace such negative attitudes and behavior patterns will not hesitate to violate your feelings or your person just to bring a small measure of twisted pleasure to themselves -- even including when it is totally at your expense.

Another area where such negative value systems are evident

is reflected in the statistics for crimes in general, and for personal assaults in particular: both statistics are up sharply not just in the United States, but also worldwide.

Yet another area where such negative value systems are evident is in certain businesses in which "meeting the bottom line" is much more important than the health and happiness of their employees. Of course, this tends to produce job stress, as well as dissatisfaction and only superficial company loyalty amongst the employees. -- Good management practices would follow a diametrically opposed strategy because, long-term, employee satisfaction and loyalty are key to maximizing a company's profits.

The substantial presence of negative value systems afflicts not just the United States, but also every major industrialized country, and many of the other cultures around the globe. **One of your major jobs is to help spread the word and the world of total inner peace** to all that you can.

Tips on Obtaining and Retaining Your Inner Peace

You will obtain inner **Peace** only indirectly -- specifically by following the steps of **Principles 1-7**. Also, realize that obtaining inner **Peace** is a journey -- and it has not a simple, highly discreet end point.

Let's review **Principles 1-7** in a condensed form.

1. Your journey to **Peace** requires knowing (to greater or lesser extent) _your_ **Purpose** -- because **Purpose** helps you move with strength, conviction, and confidence in the direction of **Peace** and fulfillment of your life blueprint.

2. By maintaining a **Positive Attitude** and surrounding yourself with positive friends, you keep your brain and your soul pointed in a forward, progressive, hopeful direction that helps keep you on an even keel so that you are much more efficient and productive in all that you do.

3. By regularly **Praying** to God, you are better able to maintain a proper focus on the items most important to fulfilling your life blueprint.

4. By successfully dealing with **Pressure**, and also taking all of the proper steps to optimize your **Preparation** for your path in life, you are much more likely to maximize your ultimate **Performance** in life. And, by **always striving to "give your best,"** you will find that your **Performance** will be enhanced, and also any stress and anxiety in your life will be greatly reduced.

5. Once you have laid a strong foundation for **1 through 4,** you will be in the strongest position to **Pass It On** with authority and strident confidence, and perhaps even with a good measure of charisma. When you **Pass It On** with the proper mindset, you will not fear reprisal, nor will you ever expect anything in return for your kind and generous acts.

6. As was indicated in Chapter 8, **your reputation and your spirit will live on forever once your physical body passes.** One of your jobs on Earth is to do everything within your power to ensure that your reputation and spirit are of the highest caliber. Your reputation and spirit are not end points that you specifically focus on; on the contrary, if your spirit and your reputation are great, that merely means that you have mastered the foundational, preceding principles.

Think of it this way: To do otherwise would tarnish the spirits of such greats as Abraham Lincoln, Jesus, the Apostle Paul, Mohammed, Gandhi, Booker T. Washington, Dr. Mary McCloud Bethune and Dr. Martin Luther King -- to name a few.

My highest hope, and the frequent desire expressed in many of my prayers, is that you make a _very_ "grand entrance" into the process of getting your life fully on track to fulfilling your life blueprint by **taking your first step today!**

Exercises

1. Write down how you imagine you will feel once you are totally at peace with yourself. -- And save it for future reading -- especially for when you finally "arrive!"

----

2. Write down what you believe people who know you will say when your physical body _actually_ passes (presumably at a much future date!).

Epilogue

Writing this book has been a labor of love. -- I hope that you have enjoyed reading it and improving your life.

If you faithfully follow the prescriptions of the **8 Principles**, you ***will:***

1. realize your life blueprint,

2. be happier and more fulfilled than you are now,

3. become a force that cannot be ignored -- because your full potential will be unleashed in all of its awesome power and glory! and

4. achieve a deeper spirituality as you help more and more people who need *you* and your help!

Notes

Notes

Notes

www.ingramcontent.com/pod-product-compliance
Lightning Source LLC
Chambersburg PA
CBHW070106100426
42743CB00012B/2658